LEAGUE UNLIMITED

ACH HOWARD collection cover artist

UPERMAN created by **JERRY SIEGEL** and **JOE SHUSTER**
y special arrangement with the **Jerry Siegel** family

POCUS

RACHEL GLUCKSTERN
TOM PALMER JR.
MICHAEL WRIGHT
Editors - Original Series
JEANINE SCHAEFER
Assistant Editor - Original Series
JEB WOODARD
Group Editor - Collected Editions
ROBIN WILDMAN
Editor - Collected Edition
STEVE COOK
Design Director - Books
AMIE BROCKWAY-METCALF
Publication Design
KATE DURRÉ
Publication Production

BOB HARRAS
Senior VP - Editor-in-Chief, DC Comics

DANIEL CHERRY III
Senior VP - General Manager
JIM LEE
Publisher & Chief Creative Officer
BOBBIE CHASE
VP - Global Publishing Initiatives & Digital Strategy
DON FALLETTI
VP - Manufacturing Operations & Workflow Management
LAWRENCE GANEM
VP - Talent Services
ALISON GILL
Senior VP - Manufacturing & Operations
HANK KANALZ
Senior VP - Publishing Strategy & Support Services
DAN MIRON
VP - Publishing Operations
NICK J. NAPOLITANO
VP - Manufacturing Administration & Design
NANCY SPEARS
VP - Sales
JONAH WEILAND
VP - Marketing & Creative Services
MICHELE R. WELLS

JUSTICE LEAGUE UNLIMITED: HOCUS POCUS

DC Comics, 2900 West Alameda Ave., Burbank, CA 91505
Printed by LSC Communications, Crawfordsville, IN, USA. 12/25/20.
First Printing.
ISBN: 978-1-77950-754-9
Library of Congress Cataloging-in-Publication Data is available.

CONTENTS

CHAPTER 1: POSTCARD FROM THE EDGE

JUSTICE LEAGUE
UNLIMITED

POSTCARD FROM THE EDGE

ADAM BEECHEN — writer CARLO BARBERI — pencils WALDEN WONG — inks
PAT BROSSEAU — letters HEROIC AGE — colors BEN CALDWELL — cover artist
JEANINE SCHAEFER — assistant editor TOM PALMER JR — editor

9

AQUAMAN DIDN'T MEET US, WHICH I THOUGHT WAS WEIRD SINCE WE'RE HERE FOR *HIS* PARTY.

BUT I'VE HEARD HE'S KIND OF A *JERK*, SO MAYBE THAT'S NORMAL.

THE LITTLE DOODAD THAT THE *ATOM* AND *STEEL* CAME UP WITH THAT LETS US *BREATHE* AND *COMMUNICATE* UNDERWATER WORKS GREAT.

MY *COSMIC CONVERTER BELT* KEEPS THE PRESSURE FROM *CRUSHING* ME, AND *SUPERMAN*, *WONDER WOMAN* AND *STEEL* DON'T EVEN NOTICE IT.

I WISH YOUR *S.T.R.I.P.E.* ARMOR HADN'T BEEN DAMAGED BY VANDAL SAVAGE.

EVEN THOUGH I *COMPLAIN* ABOUT HAVING MY *STEPDAD* AROUND, IT'D BE NICE TO HAVE YOU HERE.

ATLANTIS IS *WEIRD*. DID YOU KNOW THEY ONLY EAT *KELP* AND *SEAWEED*?

AND EXCEPT FOR AQUAMAN, EVERYBODY HERE HAS SHORT *HAIR*. IT'D GET IN THEIR *EYES* ALL THE TIME, OTHERWISE.

AND THE PEOPLE ARE ALL SO *HEAVY*. I GUESS BECAUSE OF THE PRESSURE.

WHEN I TRIED TO SIT BEFORE AQUAMAN GOT THERE, ONE GUY TOOK MY ARM AND HE FELT LIKE A *REDWOOD TREE*!

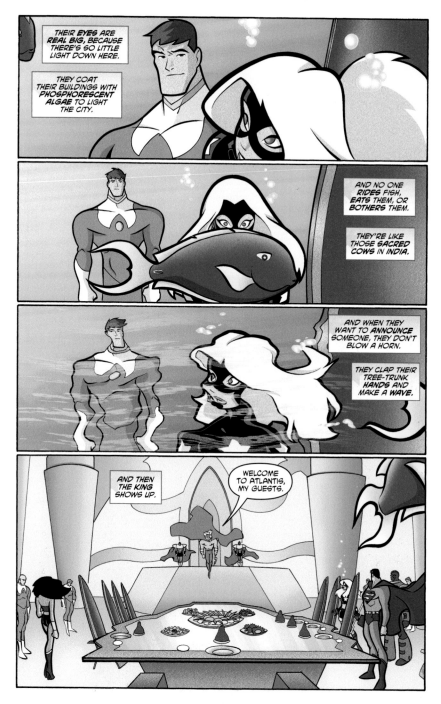

THANK YOU FOR BEARING WITH THIS SILLY RITUAL OF OURS.

IT'S *HARDLY* SILLY, AQUAMAN!

IT'S THE ANNIVERSARY OF THE DAY YOU BECAME KING OF ATLANTIS!

IT'S CAUSE FOR *CELEBRATION!*

ARIONITE CULTISTS HAVE SWORN TO RETURN ATLANTIS TO THE *OLD WAYS,* *VIOLENTLY,* IF NECESSARY.

THERE ARE MORE *IMPORTANT* THINGS TO DO THAN CELEBRATE.

AND *THAT'S* WHEN I OPENED MY *BIG FAT MOUTH.*

C'MON, YOUR HIGHNESS...ALL WORK AND NO PLAY MAKES THE KING A *DULL BOY,* RIGHT?

I DON'T BELIEVE WE'VE MET.

AQUAMAN, THIS IS *STARGIRL*. SHE'S ONE OF OUR *NEWER, YOUNGER* MEMBERS.

PLEASE TELL HER THAT *CHILDREN* DO NOT *SPEAK* UNTIL THEY ARE PROVEN WORTHY OF AN *ADULT VOICE.*

OKAY, PAT, I KNOW THE *SMART* THING WOULD HAVE BEEN TO JUST *SHUT UP* AND ALL...

BUT THIS GUY DOESN'T *KNOW* ME, OR WHAT I'VE *DONE*, OR WHAT I *CAN* DO!

I MEAN, WHAT'S SO *GREAT* ABOUT HIM? HE CAN *SWIM REAL FAST?* HE CAN *BREATHE* UNDERWATER?

HE'S PROBABLY SUCH A *CREEP* BECAUSE HE KNOWS HE'S NO SUPERMAN OR GREEN LANTERN!

AND I WASN'T GOING TO LET SOMEBODY LIKE THAT PUSH ME AROUND!

SO I OPENED MY BIG FAT MOUTH *AGAIN.*

OH YEAH?! AND WHAT WOULD *MAKE* ME WORTHY...?

BEING ABLE TO *TALK* TO *FISH?!?!*

PRETTY SMOOTH, HUH?

I FELT LIKE *DIRT*. I WANTED SO BAD TO *APOLOGIZE*...

AT THE CORONATION DINNER, THE KINGDOM'S *SEER* PRESENTS HIS *VISION* FOR THE COMING YEAR...

...A NOD TO ATLANTIS'S HERITAGE OF *MAGIC*.

...BUT THE *LAST* THING I WAS GONNA DO WAS SPEAK UP AGAIN.

...AND HERE HE IS NOW. WHAT SAY YOU, FEALL WHALESONG?

MY LIEGE...

...I BRING *DREAD TIDINGS! DISASTER* AWAITS THE KINGDOM!

HMPH. LAST YEAR, HE PREDICTED A RAIN OF *SEA URCHINS* AND--

15

16

AFTER THE QUAKE WAS OVER, AQUAMAN CHECKED IN WITH HIS SCIENTISTS.

ARE YOU ALL RIGHT, COURTNEY?

HUH? OH, YEAH, NONE OF THAT FALLING RUBBLE HIT ME.

THAT'S NOT WHAT I MEAN.

YES, YOU OVERREACTED TO WHAT AQUAMAN SAID, BUT YOU WEREN'T TOTALLY OUT OF LINE.

I WASN'T?

OCCASIONALLY, AQUAMAN GETS SO BUSY BEING A *KING* OR A *SUPERHERO,* HE FORGETS TO BE A *PERSON.*

ON OUR SECOND MISSION, HE WAS SO *CONDESCENDING* TO ME...

...I TOLD HIM HE WAS AS *PUFFED-UP* AS A *BLOWFISH!*

NO *WAY!* WHAT DID HE SAY TO *THAT?!*

NOTHING. AND IN TIME, I GOT TO KNOW *HIM,* AND HE GOT TO KNOW *ME,* AND WHAT'S PAST WAS *PAST.*

YOU'VE ONLY JUST MET. FOCUS ON YOUR JOB AND GIVE THE REST *TIME.*

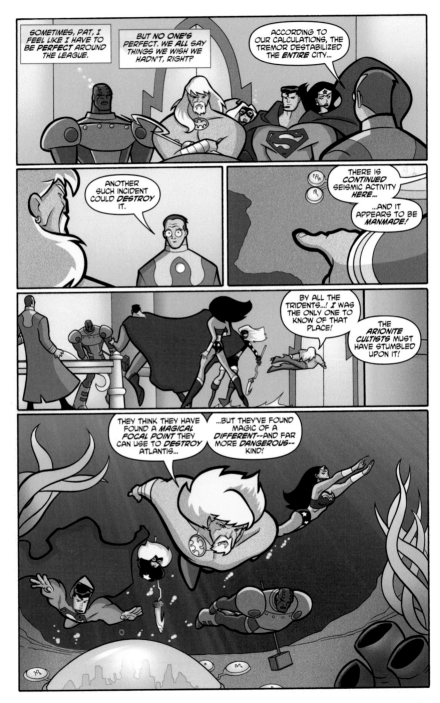

RISE, GREAT WAVES! TOPPLE, O CORAL!

RETURN TO US THE MAGIC OF OUR FATHERS, THE MAGIC OF ARION!

WHOA! WHAT'S STONEHENGE DOING DOWN HERE?

THE FORMATION IS A BROTHER TO STONEHENGE...

...FOR LIKE THAT STONE CIRCLE, THIS ONE IS ALSO A MAGIC PRISON!

A PRISON? A PRISON FOR WHAT?

ONE OF THE OLD DEMONS, STEEL...

ONE THAT WALKED THE EARTH BEFORE MAN WAS BORN!

HE HAS THE POWER TO DESTROY EVERYTHING, AND AFTER MILLENNIA OF IMPRISONMENT, THAT WILL SURELY BE HIS GOAL! FOR TODAY...

21

24

I CAN'T BELIEVE I ACTUALLY *SAID* IT.

I CAN'T BELIEVE HE ACTUALLY *LISTENED.*

I DIDN'T KNOW IF MY BELT COULD *TAKE* SO MUCH ENERGY, BUT THERE WASN'T *TIME* FOR ANY TEST RUNS.

I JUST HAD TO HOPE FOR THE *BEST.*

...AND FOCUS ON THE *JOB.*

ZZZAM

AAAAARGHHH!!!

I COULD FEEL THE BELT STRAINING TO HOLD ITS POWER.

BUT I WOULDN'T LET IT QUIT.

THE LEAGUE WAS DEPENDING ON ME.

A WHOLE CITY WAS DEPENDING ON ME.

MAYBE EVEN THE WHOLE *WORLD.*

I *WASN'T* GOING TO LET THEM DOWN.

PPPPOWWWERRRR... WHERRE ISS MYYY PPPPOWWWERRRR...?!?!

I JUST *HOPED* AQUAMAN WOULD BE READY.

DONE!

NNNNOOOOOOO!!!

NOTHING TO IT.

BUT PAT, BEATING *UMBRA* WASN'T THE *BEST* PART...

THE BEST PART WAS AQUAMAN'S CORONATION DAY SPEECH.

...AND SO, FOR HER SERVICE TO ATLANTIS...

...AND FOR TEACHING A STUBBORN KING THAT *EVERYONE* HAS SOMETHING TO OFFER...

...I DECLARE STARGIRL AN *HONORARY CITIZEN* OF OUR REALM!

OKAY, THE CULTISTS GOT AWAY, BUT IT'LL BE AWHILE BEFORE THEY TRY ANYTHING AGAIN.

SO THAT WAS MY FIRST TRIP TO ATLANTIS. NOT *BAD*, HUH?

I GUESS I BETTER MAIL THIS NOW... IF ATLANTIS HAS MAILBOXES, THAT IS.

I GUESS I HADN'T THOUGHT ABOUT THAT.

OH, WELL. NOBODY'S PERFECT.

LOVE, COURTNEY.

THE END

CHAPTER 2: EVERYBODY LIMBO!

JUSTICE LEAGUE
UNLIMITED

SAID THAT OUT *LOUD*, DIDN'T I...?

SORRY, GUYS...IT'S ME, *DEADMAN!*

I'M JUST *BORROWING* WONDER WOMAN'S *BOD* FOR A SEC 'CUZ I NEED YOUR *HELP*...

WHAT'S THE *PROBLEM*, DEADMAN?

DEADMAN...?

DEADMAN'S A *CIRCUS ACROBAT* WHO WAS *MURDERED* AND NOW HELPS A BEING NAMED *RAMA KUSHNA* MAINTAIN THE *SPIRITUAL BALANCE* OF THE UNIVERSE BY *POSSESSING* HUMAN FORMS AND ASSISTING SOULS IN NEED.

OH. SURE.

IT'S THOSE *KOOKY DEMONS THREE*...ABNEGAZAR, RATH AND GHAST?

THEY'VE TAKEN OVER *LIMBO!*

THE TRENCHCOAT BRIGADE...?

DOCTOR OCCULT, ZATANNA, DOCTOR FATE, ETRIGAN THE DEMON AND ZAURIEL, LEAGUE MEMBERS WITH STRONG TIES TO THE SUPERNATURAL.

WELL, THIS IS *MOST* OF 'EM, AT LEAST...

OH. SURE.

=SIGH= I SHOULDA KNOWN *HE* WOULDN'T'VE SHOWN UP...

YOU SHOULD HAVE MORE *FAITH*, LITTLE SPIRIT. FOR WHILE MY DUTIES OFTEN MEAN I *CANNOT* INVOLVE MYSELF IN MISSIONS SUCH AS *THESE*...

...OCCASIONALLY, *STRANGER* THINGS HAVE HAPPENED.

DEADMAN... ARE YOU *SURE* WE CAN'T HELP?

THANKS, BATS... I KNOW YOU ALL HAVE BOLDLY GONE WHERE NO FANCY-UNDERWEAR TYPES HAVE GONE *BEFORE*...

...BUT WE'RE GONNA HAVE TO *EXORCISE* THESE YAHOOS OUT OF LIMBO, NOT *PUNCH* 'EM OUT.

HERE'S WONDER WOMAN BACK... I'LL SEE YOU GUYS DOWN THE ROAD... ONE WAY OR ANOTHER...

I REALLY APPRECIATE YOU GUYS COMING ALONG...

SOMETIMES IT SEEMS/ THAT *BALANCE* ISN'T BEST/ PERHAPS IT IS TIME/ TO PUT *DARKNESS* TO THE TEST?

ABNEGAZAR, RATH AND GHAST ARE *MINOR* ANNOYANCES...

WE WILL *RESTORE* THE BALANCE BETWEEN *CHAOS* AND *ORDER* WITH EASE!

IT IS AS I SAID, HE *CANNOT* BE TRUSTED!

HE WILL *SURRENDER* US TO THE *FORCES OF EVIL* AT HIS FIRST OPPORTUNITY!

CREATURE WITH WINGS/ THOU *IDIOT* THING...

36

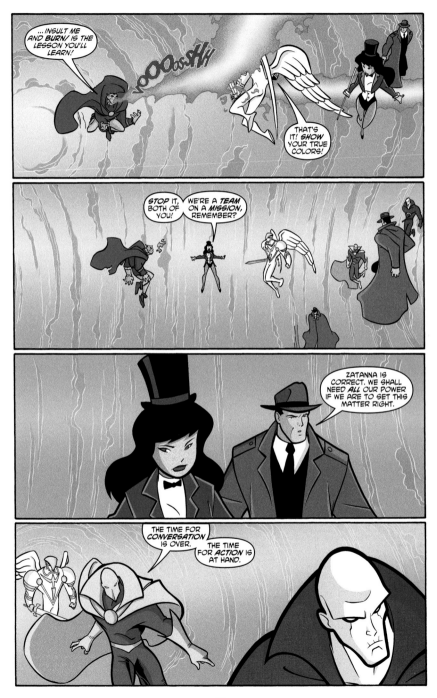

38

39

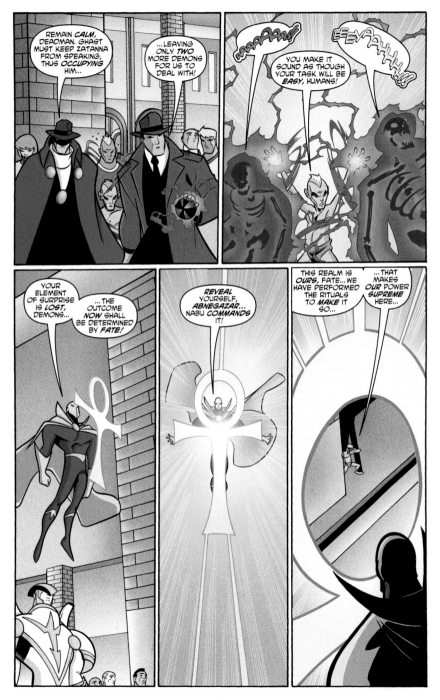

40

42

44

45

ENOUGH OF THIS WAITING! LET US BEGIN...

48

49

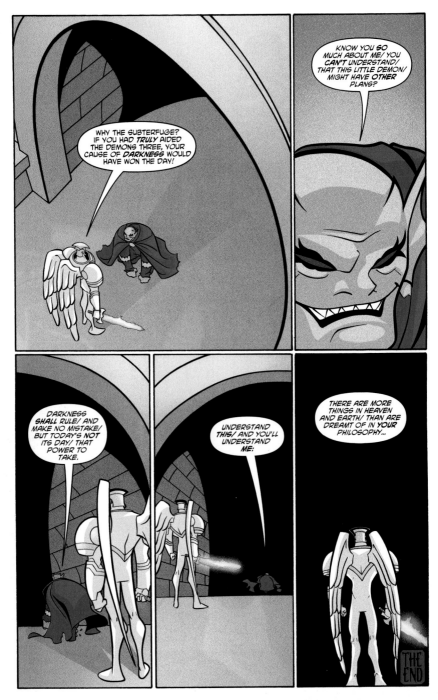

50

CHAPTER 3: THE DEVIL MAY CARE

JUSTICE LEAGUE
UNLIMITED

THE DEVIL MAY CARE

ADAM BEECHEN - script
RICK BURCHETT - art
MIKE SELLERS - letters
HEROIC AGE - colors
TY TEMPLETON - cover art
MICHAEL WRIGHT - editor

DON'T HURT ME! MOMMY, MAKE HIM STAY AWAY!!!

54

ENTER *FREELY,* DANIEL CASSIDY...

...FATE *WELCOMES* YOU.

GEE, DOC, HOW'D YOU GET ALL THIS *STUFF* IN *HERE?*

THE *ENTRANCE* TO MY *QUARTERS* IS A *PORTAL* TO MY *TOWER* IN *SALEM,* BLUE DEVIL....

...BUT *SURELY* YOU DID NOT COME HERE TO DISCUSS *HOME DECORATION*...?

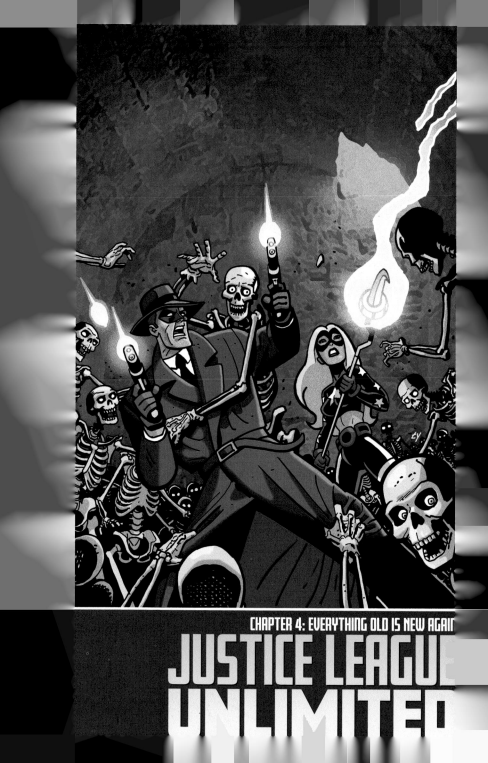

CHAPTER 4: EVERYTHING OLD IS NEW AGAIN

JUSTICE LEAGUE
UNLIMITED

EVERYTHING OLD IS NEW AGAIN

JASON HALL-WRITER　　CARLO BARBERI-PENCILLER　　BOB PETRECCA-INKER
ROBERT CLARK JR.-LETTERER　　HEROIC AGE-COLORIST　　RACHEL GLUCKSTERN-EDITOR

CHAPTER 5: HARD SPIRITS

JUSTICE LEAGUE
UNLIMITED

107

110

112

114

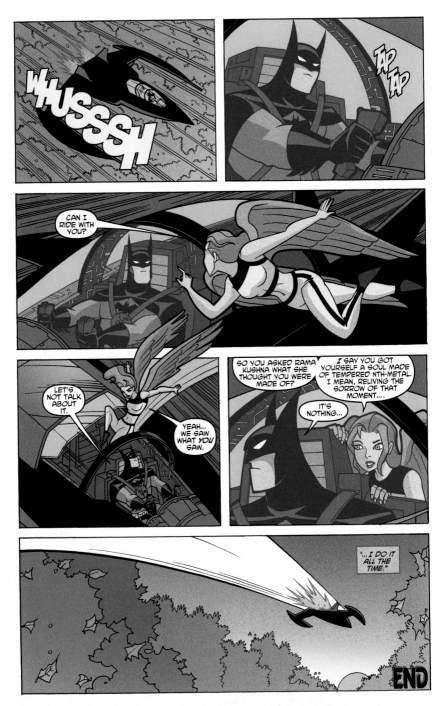

CHAPTER 6: CAST NO SHADOW

JUSTICE LEAGUE UNLIMITED

133

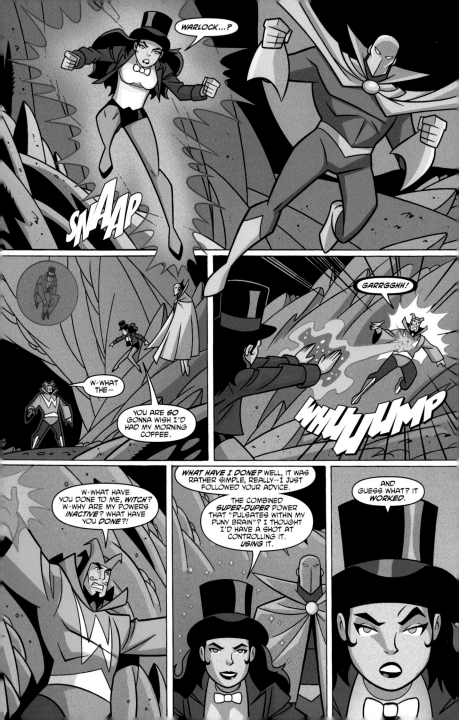

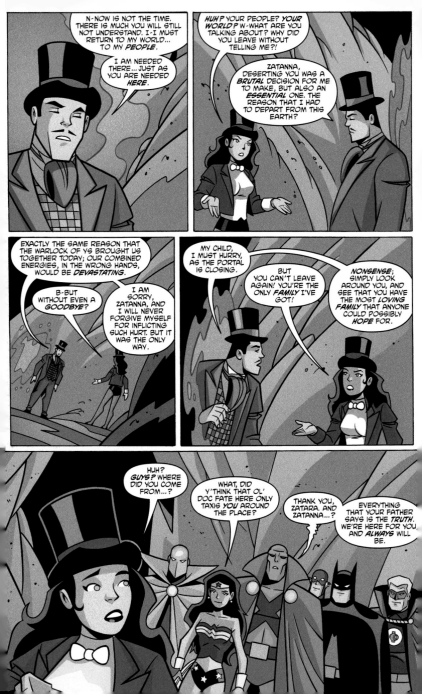

What? This is a letter from Mom!
My dearest love,
Thank you for the latest news about our daughter.
I miss her so, but I know you are doing the best you can without me.
It's hard being a single fath
a teenage girl, but
doing a wonderful job
She called me a *teenage* girl?
Wait, she's... alive?

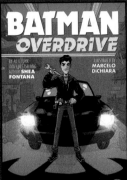

BATMAN: OVERDRIVE
Shea Fontana
Marcelo DiChiara

Teenager Bruce Wayne puts his
detective skills to the test in one of
his first adventures before becoming
Batman as he investigates who
is responsible for the murder
of his parents.

ISBN: 978-1-4012-8356-8

BATMAN TALES:
ONCE UPON A CRIME
Derek Fridolfs
Dustin Nguyen

Batman and his friends explore four
fairy-tale lands in this book by the
Batman: Li'l Gotham team!

ISBN: 978-1-4012-8340-7

DIANA: PRINCESS OF
THE AMAZONS
Shannon Hale
Dean Hale
Victoria Ying

Diana knows firsthand it is tough to be
the only kid around, but creating her
own friend may have been more than
she bargained for.

ISBN: 978-1-4012-9111-2

TEEN TITANS GO!
TO CAMP!
Sholly Fisch
Marcelo DiChiara
and more!

Robin is ready to be the Camper of
the Year, but is Apokolips ready for
the Teen Titans?

ISBN: 978-1-77950-317-6

SUPERMAN
OF SMALLVILLE
Art Baltazar
Franco

Clark Kent must learn to be Super!

ISBN: 978-1-4012-8392-6